It's All About You!

Ten Leadership Parables for Maximizing Middle Management

Charles Retts

SULIS
P R E S S

An Imprint of Sulis International Press
Los Angeles | London

IT'S ALL ABOUT YOU! TEN LEADERSHIP PARABLES
FOR MAXIMIZING MIDDLE MANAGEMENT
Copyright ©2020 by Charles Retts. All rights reserved.

ISBN (print): 978-1-946849-86-1
ISBN (eBook): 978-1-946849-87-8

Published by
An Imprint of Sulis International
Los Angeles | London

www.sulisinternational.com

\

Contents

Dedication

I dedicate this book to the best leadership professor that I ever had the privilege of knowing and working with. After spending his career with Hewlett-Packard, Rodney V. Smith M.S.L received his leadership training from the very best, and he passed that knowledge on to me.

Over the years, Rod modeled good leadership to the adjunct university faculty he worked with, sharing everything that he researched and designed concerning effective leadership. His intent was for his students to get the best education on leadership that could be given, regardless of the source. Knowing Rod during his life was truly a gift, and made me a much better person, professional, and leader. Sometimes it's the most meaningful things in life that you never see coming.

I would also like to thank author Kris Tualla for her professional and personal support throughout the writing and editing of this book. Writing a first book is a process which you are unsure you can actually finish. Having the right support, as well as professional guidance and expertise, was critical.

My wife Libbie and kids Christopher and Kaelie were also a constant encouragement, over the years, in terms of actually making sure that I didn't get stuck at the place where I was always telling people, "I am writing a book" versus "I have finished a book!"

Why Middle Management?

Lunch Can Be More Than A Vending Machine

Anyone currently in a supervisory or middle management position, doesn't have a lot of time to read. For that reason, I created this short, interactive workbook, designed to work through at your own pace. One important lesson, which I learned when training and consulting Nurse Leaders in health care, is that no one in management has the luxury of consistent breaks during the day, and lunch is usually from the nearest vending machine. They are so busy helping others, that taking care of themselves is seldom a priority.

For the past ten years, my clients, family and students have been asking me to write this book. I hesitated because I felt that there were already far too many leadership books sitting on the shelves unread! But I finally decided to write my stories because I grew frustrated by all of the talk about poor leadership in various organizations, and saw the need for honest discussion around leadership.

In spite of the endless talk, I haven't seen any real changes in how executive management is supporting middle management in order to make their working environment better. I am bombarded weekly—yes, weekly—by adult professionals who say they are not being valued and/or fully utilized by their organizations. This lack of value or utilization leads to these professionals' experiencing high levels of discouragement.

But in defiance of this endemic lack of support, and massive employee disengagement, middle management continues to be the glue that holds every organization together.

I wrote this book for those who have told me that my own journey in leadership—as articulated through my experiences and parables—not only makes sense, but the stories are authentic and come from real work challenges which they can relate to and learn from. I was also encouraged to write this book because I know that those who will read it, and are working in middle management, are the exact audience which I have a passion to help and encourage.

Those men and women working in leadership positions are the professionals in today's corporate world who actually care about others. They are not out to rule the world, and they truly believe that treating others with respect and concern should be the norm in the workplace. I am guessing that, if you are reading this book, you are as frustrated with the current state of employee disengagement as I have been.

Middle management workers are, by definition, smack in the middle of all the challenges in their organization, and being in the middle is really tough. These managers are the ones that take all the grief about organizational decisions concerning their employees, but which they have little or nothing to do with.

In addition, they have little to no input into policy, and do not receive perks that might provide a financial reason for staying in the middle and taking all that grief.

And, to make the situation even worse, based on the thousands of stories I have heard from middle management, their companies are actually more afraid of their employees than they have ever been in the past. The basis for this statement comes from middle management workers themselves. They report that executive management today is more reluctant than ever to hold employees accountable, yet they expect middle managers to do exactly that.

The information in this book is certainly not a silver bullet! But it does contain the most important leadership principles which I have learned during my thirty-year leadership journey.

The interactive leadership reflection questions are formed from the authentic "what really happened" account of my journey, which I am happy to relate did end successfully—although not without frustration, lost sleep, pain, failures and successes. If I can save anyone else from just a little of this then it will be worth the effort and time it took to write this book.

All of this experience, combined with a doctorate in adult learning, taught me how to positively influence the behavior of professional adults.

This book is also about taking the time to reflect on the professional leader that you currently are, and how you would like to deliberately impact those people which you will supervise in the future. My goal for this reflection is to confirm the person that you want to be as leader, through one conversation or situation at a time.

As you read and think about each presented parable and corresponding situation, stop and think about how you would have responded to that same situation in your current organization. This is not a "right" or "wrong" exercise, but is an opportunity for you to reflect on the leader you currently are, and the leader you truly want to be.

My hope is that this book can give you a clear perspective on the behaviors I describe as a result of my leadership journey. I want you to assess your own current leadership style, and be sincerely engaged in the outcome and impact at the end of each chapter. My goal was to create a book that would not be a quick read, but be thoughtfully worked through over time.

This book will provide simple behaviors and skills which will enable managers to create the desired environment where they and others want to work. Where others in the organization desire to do their best.

Where employees are not dominated by bullies and actively disengaged employees.

And—where we can be excited about working alongside men and women, enabled to do their best, and who want to reach their personal and professional potential. A highly professional culture where co-workers see themselves as a high-performing team actually having fun in the midst of all the rapid, crazy change.

Most of all, I want to give middle-management men and women hope. These stories might even provide increased courage to get out of bed in the morning, and face tough work-related situations with a renewed confidence armed with realistic, proven tools.

I want to emphasize that my leadership learning expressed in this book is spread over many different types of organizations, some union and some non-union, and that is why I believe the common denominator and major contributing factor in being a successful leader is YOU!

My hope is that, after working through this book, you realize the influence you do have—today—to change your work world, and that you understand there is much more to your position (lunch) than a vending machine (the status quo).

PARABLE ONE

Life Changing Leadership Is All About You

During my first month in a new leadership assignment I discovered, via the supervisors reporting to me, that the current employee culture was not very leadership supportive. This was created in part by past management and in part as a result of being a long-time union environment. I was warned ahead of time that I would not be welcomed as the new manager with anything resembling open arms.

One day, about a month in, I was visited by an employee who bolted into my office, did not bother to introduce himself, and immediately announced to me that he was a long-term employee of my department who had outlasted numerous managers over the years. He also stated that (given the average management span in that particular culture) he would be in the department longer than I would, and that no matter what I did during my tenure that he was not going to work any harder for me than he had worked for any of the previous managers.

At this point he launched into a five-minute monologue, lecturing me on everything that was wrong both with the leadership and the overall department. To make the situation even more awkward, one of my supervisors was in my office at the time and witnessed the entire diatribe.

STOP FOR A MOMENT

Please take a minute right now to reflect on this situation and write down a few words that would define what you would be thinking if you were the leadership in this situation, and/or how you would have responded to this encounter in your current organization. Be aware, this employee's position in the company happened to be two levels below mine.

_____

_____

_____

_____

When I believed that the employee had vented all that he needed to, I politely asked if he was finished, or did he have any other information that he wanted to share with me. Key point here: I was serious and sincere in my request. The employee stared at me for a minute, said he did not, and then left my office.

At that point the supervisor who had been trapped in my office by this unexpected visit looked at me with a stunned expression on her face, and asked why I didn't do anything more aggressive to the employee who just "wandered into my office like he owned the place." She wondered why didn't I defend myself. Why I allowed an hourly employee speak to me in the way that he did.

In her reaction were statements such as, "you shouldn't have to take that from employees in your position" and "you do know you have the right to put him into immediate disciplinary action for his behavior."

My answer was as simple as it was brief: "Actually, that employee just did me an incredible favor. He just told me, in a matter of minutes, what could have taken me months to figure out."

This should give you a clear picture of the current culture I found myself up against.

LEADERSHIP LEARNING

When changing a culture, as the leader, your first priority is to assess the current culture. You can't change what you don't understand. Be aware that changing an entire culture of employees who have been set in their ways for their entire careers is an extremely difficult task—and it can take up to a year just to thoroughly understand the culture which has already been established.

Leaders don't allow others to dictate their behavior. How I have decided to behave as a leader will never change because of an employee's behavior. That is way too much power and influence to give to another person. I also understand that change begins *with the leader*.

In the situation which I presented, it is important to note that I killed two birds with one stone: I modeled the behavior, which I would cultivate, to both the employee and my supervisor. I could not have planned such a perfect opportunity to be an example to both of those individuals. It was the perfect storm!

What my supervisor failed to initially realize is that, although it may not have appeared that way to her, my behavior was extremely deliberate. I was actually in control of the situation the entire time. I strongly believe that being *deliberate* is one of the most important characteristics of good leaders.

Effective leaders are not "lucky" in their actions, and they do not "wing it" regardless of the situation —or their ego! Effective leaders understand who they are as a leader, and they fully understand the type of behavior which is necessary to change a currently disengaged and negative culture.

WHAT WAS I DOING—OR NOT DOING?

- Non-verbally I gave the employee respect by keeping eye contact with him throughout his angry monologue.

- I gave him respect by not interrupting what he was saying.

- My expression did not exhibit anger or confusion, and I did not squirm in my chair as if I was nervous or waiting for him to finish.

- At the end of his statement, I asked if he was finished, politely and with all the sincerity that I could muster at that moment. Even though I wanted to respond differently, I did not.

- I did not try to defend myself, or the company, or management in general. I just listened.

- I did not do all the negative things which I had the right to do as a manger because I had bigger goals in mind than winning a spontaneous confrontation. My goal was to totally change an entire departmental culture.

STOP FOR A MOMENT

What do you think was learned about the current culture that saved me tons of time in the long run? Think about it for a moment. What would you have learned about your organization from this encounter that was worth far more than standing up for yourself and acting the boss?

_____

_____

_____

_____

OTHER LESSONS LEARNED

- Employees in that department felt very protected by the union and were not concerned about what management wanted from them.

- There was very little respect for management.

- Some employees in the department harbored a great deal of anger.

- I was the enemy.

As a result of this situation, I now had an idea of the culture, and had a starting point in which to begin my culture change. I also had a good idea of what needed to be changed.

STOP FOR A MOMENT

When was the last time you took a day, an hour, or even a few minutes, to think about the person you have become in life, and the person that you want to be in leadership? Have you ever written a personal vision for your life? If you are in leadership, this is not an option. You could be damaging adults in your current position and not even know it—but your employees do.

Maybe you shouldn't be in leadership at all, if you are only in it for the money, prestige, or just because you were asked to be. Begin today by writing down some thoughts on the following lines that define *what kind of person you want to be at the very CORE of your life.*

Understand this truth: your words and your behavior should intentionally and deliberately reflect your definition!

_____

_____

_____

_____

KEY POINT

Culture drives employee performance, and successful leaders deliberately create their own culture. Cultures are created one parable, one deliberate conversation, and one unexpected encounter at a time. Take advantage of those moments! Knowing yourself, and knowing who you want to be as a leader, should be your *number one priority*.

Life Changing Leadership really is all about YOU!

PARABLE TWO

Look for the Gold in Your Own Mine

So often in leadership, the first thing that comes to mind when wanting to change a department's culture is to look outside the department for new talent. We tend to forget that it's very possible we already have currently underutilized employees who would be willing to be that "new" talent.

I was asked, at one point in my career, to manage a professional group of employees in customer service. During the first few weeks of being the new manager, I lined up one-on-one employee conversations with each member of my staff, in order to go deeper into both who I was going to be as their "leader", and to learn more about them.

While having these interviews I met with one employee who had been put into discipline by the previous manager for not being more engaged within the organization. As in any disciplinary process, termination was the possible final destination, if "Maria" did not improve and show more commitment to providing leadership within the department.

I mentioned to Maria that, even though I was her new manager, I was not going to remove her from the disciplinary process. She was going to continue to be on the discipline train, as I call it. I explained to her that this process/train would include occasionally meeting with me one-on-one in order to discuss her performance and behavior.

During our conversations over the following weeks, I was trying to discover as much information as I could in terms of Maria's potential skills and abilities, which could then be utilized by the department. As a result of this process I felt that, even though she was in discipline, Maria was a strong player in the department and would be a significant loss if she left the company.

For this reason, a feasible option could be to find a better departmental fit for her, rather than removing her completely from the organization. Also, Maria was a long-term employee with the company, so I was beginning to question why, at this point in her career, she found herself in this particular situation.

At the end of one of our weekly meetings, in a move of desperation, I randomly asked her to develop a comprehensive resume for our next meeting which included her entire adult professional work history—inside and outside this current company.

To be honest, I had absolutely no idea what I was going to do with this document at the time of my request. But a few weeks later, as requested, Maria brought me an extremely detailed and comprehensive work history. In fact, I was a little sorry I asked her to do it, given the size of the manuscript.

What do they say in management? Be careful what you ask for! Little did I know that this request would begin a significant learning curve on my part, one that would stay with me for the rest of my leadership career.

After reading Maria's complete work history, one thing was clear: this particular employee, regardless of her current employment at our company, clearly had proven engagement and leadership skills outside the company.

STOP FOR A MOMENT

Please take a minute to reflect on this situation and write down a few words that would define what you would be thinking if you were the leader in this situation. How might you have responded to this employee, given what you now understand about their experience? What would you say or do in your next one-on-one?

_____

_____

_____

_____

During our next performance session, I simply asked the obvious question, "Why are you in discipline for not showing more engagement, commitment, or leadership in our company?"

The startling answer was, "I was never asked to by my former supervisor."

LEADERSHIP LEARNING

Being a successful manager in leadership means that you are moving forward—not that you always know exactly *what* you are moving toward! So many successful decisions in my leadership career came from simply taking steps forward in a situation, without knowing what the specific outcome was going to be. The key is to understand that, whatever you are doing, you are doing for the right reasons.

Given this situation it was clear to me that managers may not necessarily have a clear picture of who they have reporting to them! If this is true then how can any of us truly utilize the diversity we have in our organizations if we are *not even aware* of all the skills and experiences of the men and women who we currently have on our staff?

After that I asked myself, "How many other employees in my department are not engaged because they have never been asked to be?"

My final question for Maria was to ask her what did I need to do in order to get her one-hundred-percent engagement and leadership in my department. She said that all I had to do was ask. So—I asked. And I got it, immediately. Needless to say, Maria completed the disciplinary process in a very positive fashion. She is still working for that organization today.

From that point on I consistently asked these two basic questions of thousands of adult professionals:

1. Do you feel *fully utilized* in your current organization?

2. Do you feel *valued* in your current department?

And for over seventy percent of those whom I asked, the answer has been a resounding *no!*

As management/leadership, how can we fully utilize and value our current employees if we do not even know who they are, or what they bring to the organization? Being too busy is no excuse for not asking.

WHAT WAS I DOING—OR NOT DOING?

- I was being authentic as a leader and truly trying to understand the value of an employee, even though I was aware of what a previous manager had done and/or thought of this employee.

- I did not assume anything about this employee given their current circumstances and was willing to make my own determination.

- I did what I felt was natural to do, even if it might not be clear in my own mind, and even if it might even seem foolish to the employee.

- I did not assume that the employee had nothing to offer the organization.

- I was willing to take a risk.

OTHER LESSONS LEARNED

- I realized that, in the past, I had never truly known very much about the employees who reported to me.

- As a leader who wanted to leverage all the diversity that I could in my own department, I began to request a brief work history resume from those who reported to me.

- I made certain that I always assessed and evaluated the skills and experiences of everyone in my own department, before I started looking outside my department or organization for new employees with specific skills and abilities.

- My first priority as a leader should always be to fully utilize and maximize the full value of my current employees.

STOP FOR A MOMENT

Take a minute to ask yourself these questions: as a leader, how much do I really know about those that I am responsible for in my organization? What one or two simple questions could I ask my employees that would educate me to the diversity of skills that they might bring to my organization or department?

_____

_____

_____

_____

KEY POINT

Sometimes leadership is simple, and sometimes we make it difficult. We may need to do some things which require a lot of time, even though we may not be sure in advance that the results will be rewarding. As many others have said before, leadership seems to be more of an art than a science—if it were just a science, it would be easy.

PARABLE THREE

Take Advantage of Surprises

If you have been in middle management for a significant amount of time, you are aware that surprises happen all the time. You have also learned that the end result has to do with *how* you approach and manage those surprises.

I am not sure who first made the statement, "Do as I say, not as I do," but the fact remains that our behavior does speak much louder than our words, and nothing we can say will ever change that.

Of course, when we are in a leadership position, we are always being watched, and our employees always observe us to see if our actions and behaviors line up with our expressed words.

If our actions do not match our words, we lose credibility and take several steps backwards in trying to be a leader. Just for the record, no one is perfect in making all of our words line up with all of our actions, so we shouldn't take too much time to recover after messing up. There will be times when we need to just take the hit to our reputations, and then keep moving forward.

At one point in my career I had the opportunity to lead yet another department that needed its performance to significantly improve. One day, after spending a lot of time in my office—I left my office to stretch my legs. I walked the hundred feet or so to the water cooler, where I picked up a cup of water, and then walked back into my office.

Doing this was not a big deal, but I had never done it before. Moments after I returned to my office, I had a supervisor come into my office and ask me if I was okay. I asked why she was asking, and she said that a number of employees were nervous about me, and the word on the floor was that I looked extremely upset. Some thought it would be better for them if they kept their distance.

I couldn't believe it. All I did was walk to the water cooler. After thinking about it, I remembered that I was probably mumbling to myself and probably didn't look very happy. And, in this particular environment, *no one* seemed to be very happy, and management was not trusted.

In another situation about a month later, I was coming back from lunch and one of my supervisors stopped me and asked me if anything was going on earlier in my office. He had been told by employees that they had seen me under my desk, and acting pretty upset, as they passed by my office. Once again, they were nervous about my behavior.

I told the supervisor that while I was out at lunch, an IT employee had been fixing my computer. The man under the desk was not me. We laughed and shrugged it off as a crazy misunderstanding.

But I began thinking about both of these situations. They were both odd and unfair assumptions about my behavior, and the rumors about me had spread quickly.

Interestingly enough, not long after these incidents, one of my friends in the organization told me that he heard a random rumor that I wore a hairpiece. I couldn't believe it!

I did have thick hair, and it hadn't yet gone gray or white. I guess some people could not believe that I could be as old as I said I was, and still have a full head of brown hair.

STOP FOR A MOMENT

Take a minute to consider these three incidents that spread throughout the department, and write down what you were thinking about while reading the stories. What would your reaction have been to these rumors? Is there something pro-active that you could do as a result of these rumors? Is there a way that you could take these unexpected situations and turn them into positive opportunities that would help you continue to change the current culture?

_____

_____

_____

LEADERSHIP LEARNING

When you are in management, you are always being watched by your employees. Every one of them is making assumptions about how you are doing, what is happening in your life, and what is going on in the department that you are managing. This is not fair, but this is what happens.

One of the most frequent challenges, which I consistently had when taking over any dysfunctional department, is managing the rumor mill. This is a common challenge for anyone trying to bring significant change into any organization.

The challenge is: can a leader get correct information out to the employees before incorrect information spreads. In my experience, if employees do not believe that they have enough information from management, then they will make things up.

One of my core values, which I developed over time as a leader, was to always over-communicate to employees, being deliberate about staying ahead of the rumor mill. I realized that I should take these three crazy rumors and turn them into an opportunity to communicate. I quickly got on my computer and emailed the entire department. I announced that, starting that day, I would send a "rumor control" email every Friday afternoon.

In the first email I announced that I did not wear a hairpiece, stating that they could come into my office and pull my hair as proof if they wished to. I also said that I was absolutely fine, and that the man on the floor under my desk was not me, it was the computer technician. I had gone to lunch.

Up to this point I had not been able to break through the lack of trust and anger that preexisted in the department. Obviously, the employees were hoping I would get fired, not because they hated me as a person, but because they did not *know* me as a person.

The response to the "rumor control" email was amazing. The staff and employees could not believe that their manager would send out a general note to the entire department because apparently this had never happened before.

Besides that, if a manager ever *would* send out an all-employee notification, it would never have been to have fun for the purposes of rumor control.

I was consistent with what I promised in terms of a rumor mill email every Friday. It was so positive and so much fun, that I decided to add information about decisions that I made the previous week, and explain how those decisions fit into the new mission and the new culture which I was hoping to develop. This one simple act of leadership engagement had a significant impact.

This rumor control/decision update email continued every Friday for four years, until I had accomplished all the goals set for this department and moved on to yet another position!

Along the way, I knew I had thoroughly accomplished my goal and vision to over-communicate with my employees with great success.

WHAT WAS I DOING—OR NOT DOING?

- I decided to listen to what was *really* happening in my department, and I seriously thought about all the rumors—even the most negative and critical comments.

- I listened to everyone who wanted to talk to me, and tried to search for something of value in whatever they were telling me, no matter how angry or misguided they were.

- I forced myself to not get angry or defensive when someone did not agree with me, but focused on listening to the points they were trying to make.

- I didn't allow situations to determine how I felt, or how I made decisions. I returned to my core values and goals.

- I took risks and did some crazy things, knowing that if those ideas did not work, I could stop them at any time and change my direction. After all, I *was* the manager.

- I began to trust that many of my staff and employees knew the business better than I did, and their knowledge and buy-in were necessary to change the negative, disengaged culture that had been previously created.

Stop for a Moment

Take a minute and think about a negative situation or unfair assumption about you or your department, or a false rumor that people have been spreading. Now take some time to brainstorm, with yourself, about ways that you could utilize that situation to create an opportunity that might help you influence employees, or support them, or support the change that you want to make in the culture in a positive way. It may take a few days to come up with a good idea if you are not used to doing this. You might also brainstorm ideas with others that you respect; perhaps your staff.

_____

_____

_____

_____

Key Point

Leading a department of adult professionals can be full of surprises, rumors, misunderstood impressions, and crazy suggestions. Take advantage of all of them, and turn them into opportunities! Good leaders are creative and deliberate in creating employee collaboration, engagement, team work, innovation, and communication.

PARABLE FOUR

Make the Unconventional Conventional

This is not a new management concept, for sure, but there is a new twist that I have discovered over the years, and that is: success does not always come to you in the way that you are expecting it to. In fact, narrow thinking and not being open to success in a different package can cause us to fail.

As discussed earlier, the first step in totally changing any culture is to assess the present culture. It is critical to figure out what is really happening day-in and day-out. For example, after spending a few months in the position of managing a new operation, employees were constantly telling me that there was an ongoing problem with our phones. Calls were being dropped, and the employees claimed that it had nothing to do with their actions.

At first, I didn't believe them, and thought it *had* to be human error. The truth was, I was so busy with other critical challenges in the start-up that I did not need another headache. I was legitimately swamped, like everyone else in middle-management.

After about three or four months, I grew tired of the complaints and decided to prove to the employees that it was, in actuality, their fault. So, I contacted the engineering department responsible for maintaining the system.

The advice from the engineers accountable for the up-keep of the telephone system was to tell the employees that this was not a systems issue, and it must be something either the customer or the phone representative was doing.

I have to be honest and admit that I believed the engineers, and not the employees. That made sense to me. After all, they were the authorities on the telephone system—and they were salaried employees. I frankly thought that this was a reasonable explanation of the problem. In fact, the director I reported to felt that there must be more to the problem than I was recognizing, but then he was much smarter and more diligent than I ever was. It does sometimes help to have a smarter boss than you are.

So many times, those of us in management do not want to take the time to be a leader. We are overwhelmed in general, and sometimes just lazy. And I confess, in this instance I was lazy—or more likely, completely overwhelmed.

Then one day I realized that the human error which was occurring was amazingly consistent. I wondered what harm could come out of believing those who were actually *on* the telephone for every minute of their working lives. I decided to take a risk and believe what the employees were saying, and question the experts concerning our systems.

I went to my boss and laid out a plan, with a budget, for us to borrow an engineer from the engineering group for six months to assess the entire system. This was definitely thinking outside the box, as nothing like this had never been done before.

The solution seemed simple enough. Having an engineer spend a few months tracking every call that came into, and out of, the center should discover what was actually happening.

Of course, there were no funds for any such project which meant the engineers would have to pick up the tab. Unfortunately, every corporate budget is important, and that does control decisions sometimes.

Not willing to give up on this problem, my next move was to knock on the door of the engineering department, laid out my plan, and asked if they had a budget to support a phone system assessment.

At this point, I reduced the request to just one dedicated engineer for two months. The answer I received was that there was nothing wrong with the phone system, and they could not spend either the time or the personnel on this project. And furthermore, if I was an engineer, I would understand.

To be honest, I did understand their argument. I had no education or experience as an engineer with communication systems, and we really did have one of the best engineering departments in the state. My background was in human resources.

STOP FOR A MOMENT

Take a minute and think about what you might have done in this situation. How would you have responded? How would you proceed in a leadership way to resolve this challenge?

_____

_____

_____

_____

Unfortunately, my immediate gut reaction was to give up and let the current organizational culture dictate my leadership.

Let me be clear: I don't believe that any leader should *ever* be a bully, disrespect, or undervalue the opinions of other professionals in the organization. That said, when you truly believe that you have a game-breaking challenge, you do need to be a defender for your employees.

Because of the type of culture I wanted to create in the company, one that was respected internally by others and not just externally with the customer, I decided to shift directions.

Be mindful that this direction did not come to me immediately. This is one reason why long-term change takes so long to create—sometimes you need to get beyond yourself to make any progress. This doesn't mean if we don't get our own way, we give up on our core values when working with other professionals in our companies.

Then I remembered that in my past meetings and conversations with the engineering group, I was introduced to an employee that did not have his engineering degree, but was hoping to go back to school to get it.

As a result, he was not getting paid engineering rates, nor was the company paying for him to go back to school to continue his engineering education. "Ted" was young, but seemed eager and passionate about his work.

Since I had not totally burned my bridges with engineering over this situation, I decided to ask about Ted and find out what the department's plans were for him. The manager admitted that he was not sure what types of projects Ted would eventually be assigned to.

I asked the manager if he would consider letting Ted work with me on the telephone issue for a short period of time. Since he was not an engineer in the department, the manager agreed to loan him to my department for the purpose of conducting phone system research for two months, and at no cost to me.

We agreed that, not only would this be a win-win situation for both of us, it would be a great experience for Ted and help his career. My manager agreed with us as well, especially since nothing would come out of our budget because Ted would continue to receive his salary from the engineering group.

I created a plan to meet with Ted every morning for him to debrief me. After that, I stuck him in a room with a telephone and plenty of flip chart pages. His job was to take notes on the calls that came into and out of the department.

I had no idea how he might best accomplish this, so I gave him the freedom to spend that time any way he wanted to. I *trusted* that he knew more about the phone system than I ever would. As a result of this win-win, I began to develop a bond with the engineering department.

The end result was amazing. Ted was able to discover that there was, in fact, a problem with the phone system at certain times of the day. Phone calls were being dropped for reasons that had nothing to do with employee or customer error.

This discovery led to my director conducting a comprehensive in-depth evaluation of the entire phone system. The repairs resulted in significantly improved productivity and employee motivation, now that this frustration was no longer an issue.

A side benefit of this entire ordeal, which was particularly rewarding for me, is that Ted—the engineering department employee who was not an engineer—became an expert concerning this phone system and understood the system better than anyone else in the company.

With his hands-on experience, he was able to discover some additional issues within the current system, ones that only he knew how to work with the phone system company to correct.

Ted established a great relationship with the phone system owners, who later offered him a position in another state at the corporate offices, at twice his current salary, with full education benefits and moving expenses.

As a leader, this was a huge win for me! Not only was I able to resolve a huge problem in my department, I also had a hand in developing another department's employee in a way that enabled him to reach his full potential. What more could anyone ask for as a leader?

Because I was flexible, and did not let my ego take over my actions, I took a risk and believed that we could eventually come to a resolution. The package that my solution came in was not what I originally expected, and was not the conventional one that I was looking for.

I could have quit at that point, but by accepting something different and not losing sight of my overall objective, I improved my credibility with both executive management and, as mentioned, the engineering department, while along the way providing a dream opportunity for an employee who was not even in my department. All I needed to do was to be willing to go with an unconventional solution.

That was not all. Being in a new culture, this was a big step in gaining credibility in my own backyard. I had eventually taken the employee perspective seriously and modeled to them the kind of culture I wanted to create. One which valued and respected everyone's opinion and perspective, even if it conflicted with my own opinion and perspective. And the union became a huge support as well!

LEADERSHIP LEARNING

Remember to look in your own backyard for the resources necessary, or a creative solution, and understand that not every solution is about money, or other departments giving up something so you can succeed. We all know that the easy solution is rarely the most impactful or rewarding. As stated, it must begin with the leader you desire to be and the culture you desire to build.

The fact is, my initial defeat meant that I was able to create *more* successes, in more areas of the company, and also in terms of building a new culture in my department, than if I had not encountered resistance.

Being a leader means being willing to take the extra steps and time necessary to uncover the truth. Frankly, it seems that being successful in leadership is more about making sure that you are doing all that you can, in every challenge that is brought to you, regardless of who is bringing it.

There is a myth that the only difference between a chunk of coal and a diamond is the pressure. It is true that in so many situations, if there were no challenges, the final result would not have been as good. *Be the diamond and not a chunk of coal.*

WHAT WAS I DOING — OR NOT DOING?

- Although my original plan was not being supported, I understood that I needed to respect the decisions being made in the organization while continuing to look for another solution.

- I respected the fact that, even though the engineering department could have taken me more seriously with this issue, I needed to respect their position and model a relationship that would last into the future—by focusing on the long-term relationship and not a short-term win.

- In both situations I was modeling the importance of "internal customer service" which is taught in every effective customer service training program, and a principal I wanted to reflect in my new culture.

- I was successful in developing an employee who was frustrated with the lack of value he had in the organization, and gave him a platform in which he could improve his value and take a step in developing his true potential.

- I was able to improve the phone system, which gained me support and credibility with both the employees and the union in the company. It also showed all of them that I could be trusted, and was serious about creating a best-in-class operation.

STOP FOR A MOMENT

What did I learn about the department and building a new culture? Think about what came to your mind as you were reading this story. What long-term results were impacted by the direction I ended up taking, rather than bucking the system?

_____

_____

_____

_____

OTHER LESSONS LEARNED

- Your employees are watching how you manage, make decisions, and treat others both in and out of your department. They really do want leadership with integrity.

- It is powerful when you utilize your own employees to build a successful new culture because they already function in the culture you are building. They are the ones that will eventually make change happen.

STOP FOR A MOMENT

Take a minute and think about a time when you were derailed in what you thought was the right approach to a problem. How did you respond? If you responded negatively and quit, think about what you could have done even if it meant taking a lot of side roads in order to get your results. What are you working on right now, that if you reconsidered your course of action for the greater good, you just might get the results you want?

_____

_____

_____

_____

KEY POINT

It is powerful in the long run to build bridges if you truly care about the total organization, and don't just stick to your original agenda. This can be a humbling experience for a leader but internal customer service pays off big dividends and can be a super strong foundation for building your new culture. Do not leave it out of your formula!

PARABLE FIVE

Leadership is Actually Pretty Simple

If you have been in management or leadership for a while, then it may have occurred to you that many of the ideas which you've had about changing your department, or influencing employees to be more engaged in their jobs, were ideas that were surprisingly uncomplicated.

In fact, they were surprisingly simple!

The flip-side to this statement is that life changing leadership is not easy. Successful leadership takes a concentrated effort and a significant amount of time.

The majority of management jobs I have had in my career demanded a good amount of improvement and change. Many of the employees in these departments were not satisfied with their jobs, had been in the department for a number of years, and were neither actively nor positively engaged. Also, many of the supervisors whom I was put in charge of had become part of the problem, and were disinclined to become a part of the solution.

It occurred to me, after leading in some challenging departments, that previous leaders in those departments which I had been assigned to had never truly engaged in *consistent, deliberate, meaningful conversations* with their employees or supervisors.

It seems that those of us in management are always talking about how important communication is in changing departmental or employee behavior, but as management, how often do we take the time to have meaningful conversations with disengaged employees and supervisors? How can we fix things if we don't truly understand the employees' and staff's current motivation and/or career goals?

I believe that the majority of men and women in management positions would agree that the most important element in changing an organization or department is having the *right* people on your management staff. The leadership books, which I have referenced over the years as an adjunct faculty member, discuss this critical factor—yet they don't explain how to make it happen.

Over the years, more than half of professional adults in management positions have told me that they are not supported in their organization in terms of holding employees accountable, putting those employees on the discipline train, or if necessary, removing them from the organization.

Unfortunately, there is a real reason why we have so many employees today working for the company and at the same time not engaged in the company. I was told by an attorney recently that in working with Human Resource Departments the primary force he confronts is their fear of their own employees.

In addition, research and polls indicate that too many employees today are allowed to be disengaged, even to the point of bullying other members of the organization without experiencing any negative consequences.

It appears that because current organizational managers are afraid of repercussions from their own employees, that lack of follow-through creates a negative, undermining culture. It is easy for me to be critical of management, since I have been in those positions for many years. But it is also easy to understand the challenges, and just how difficult it is to take back control of your department once it has been torn apart by disengaged employees.

My point in all this is: Why aren't we, as leadership, having more direct and honest conversations with our staff? Why aren't we trying to discover their attitudes about working for us and the company? And why aren't we using that information to decide if they should even be employed in their current jobs?

One day, after moving into a new position, I was thinking about *how* to construct an entirely new culture, one which would be run by fully engaged employees. I wondered how I could meet the challenge of assessing a new staff that I had never met—and who were very upset that I was being transferred into their area from a totally different department. Did they even want to remain in the department?

I was mentally ticking off all the suggestions I had read in leadership books, but nothing really caught my imagination.

So, I returned to my core value concerning the importance of management having deliberate, honest and meaningful conversations with their staff. I wondered what might happen if I arranged to meet with each of my future supervisors before I actually began working as their manager.

Would they be agreeable to this? What would I talk about? What would I say the reason was for this early meeting?

Of course, I didn't have answers to any of these questions, but I decided to try it anyway, because doing so would begin to model the leadership and communication style that I wanted to restore to this department.

The simple solution was to call each of my supervisors and ask if they could reserve three hours to meet with me to discuss our future department. To be honest, I randomly selected three hours. I had no idea how these meetings would last five minutes, much less three hours, but I was not going to sell myself or my supervisors short.

To my surprise, I did not have a single supervisor question my request. But the real surprise for me came later; each meeting could have easily lasted four hours, and the supervisors were eager to discuss opinions, feelings and future goals—some of them even to the point of telling me why they disliked their job.

Wow! Why had I never done this before?

As a result of these meetings, I created a first level of trust with my future supervisors. We had deliberate conversations, either supporting them in leaving their current position to do what they really wanted to do in life, or supporting them in doing more for the department than they had ever been asked to do by the previous manager. My new culture had begun, and I hadn't officially moved into my position! A pretty simple and fun solution to address a suspicious, distrusting staff.

STOP FOR A MOMENT

Take a minute and write down the last time you had a conversation with your employees about their current engagement and motivation in their job, and their future goals and objectives. Have you ever had this type of in-depth conversation with your direct staff? What might happen if you did have this type of conversation with your staff? What positives might come of it? Are you afraid of doing this? And if so, why?

_____

_____

_____

_____

The simple, obvious question to be asked at this point is: "How well do you know the goals and objectives of those who are on your staff? Those whom you depend on to reach your departmental goals and objectives?"

Overall, this was an amazingly simple idea and all I had to do was take a risk in discovering, at a deep level, who was really going to be working for me. Before I even began the job of turning around a poorly performing department, I had to find out who wanted to do this with me and who did not.

Within one year I had created a totally engaged and committed team, which I needed in order to turn around the department. The professionals that left my staff not only left happily, they left wondering why every manager they ever had, had not been concerned about their goals and objectives in life. In fact, I still have relationships and coach with many of those employees today.

LEADERSHIP LEARNING

We tend to make leadership and running a department way too complicated. If I want to find out something about anyone in my department, what is keeping me from asking them?

It seems, for whatever the reason, that those of us in leadership are afraid of developing deliberate and sincere adult relationships, ones where we can have open and honest discussions.

Many in management have no clue who is really working for them, because they spend more time talking about communication than actually doing it. In leadership, it will be difficult to create a high performing department or organization if we don't create bonds with employees that are based on who they really are as people.

As a side note, I have asked professionals with whom I have worked with and taught over the years, if their company has training programs on Communication Skills and Active Listening. Back in the day, when I was manager of training, every organization that I knew of had both of these courses as primary training programs for all of their employees.

Today, these two training programs are tough to find in any organization. It is no wonder that professionals today are so bad at developing strong, sincere, honest relationships with each other.

If we want to build trusting employee relationships, we need to *return to talking in-person* and rely on texts and emails less. In my opinion, while texting and emails are great tools, they have also had a huge negative impact on our ability to communicate with each other effectively.

WHAT WAS I DOING-OR NOT DOING?

- I had decided to open up my thinking and just focus on what I wanted the culture to look like and not so much on what was wrong with the department.

- I decided that before I made any decisions or assumptions about the department, I would consult with the professionals already in the department and who knew it best.

- I was modeling, again, the type of culture I wanted to create before I even started to create it.

- I showed my direct reports that I would value their experience and honor their years with the department by making them a top priority in understanding the department.

- I began to create a bond of trust with each of my direct reports even though I had no idea if they intended to support me in developing a brand-new culture.

OTHER LESSONS LEARNED

- Building a trusting relationship with employees is a huge challenge today. Most employees will admit that they do not trust their management.

- I need to always be determined to change this so-called unchangeable attitude concerning trust, and build a strong, supportive relationship with every one of my employees.

- Think "simple."

STOP FOR A MOMENT

Take a minute and think about a time in the past when you did something that was so simple, yet it had an impact on those whom you were responsible to influence formally or informally. Write it down.

A BONUS – ANOTHER SIMPLE IDEA

If I were to create a vehicle to build trust and improved communication in a department, I would have to make my physical presence known and available to the employees whenever I was in my office. But what if my office was in a place where employees would have to go out of their way, or out of their routine in order to see me? This was the challenge in one case.

The office of a previous manager, the office I was to take over, was in a location where employees would never be able to have casual contact. As an added benefit, as he put it in a personal interview, he could also leave the office early without being seen by the employees or his staff.

He also mentioned that he was not all that interested in getting to know the employees because there were just too many of them. He left all employee relationships to his supervisors in the department.

After this conversation with the manager it was clear that, for me to have any daily contact with the employees, I would have to relocate my office closer to the middle of the department. By doing this, everyone would be able to see me by having to walk by my office on a daily basis whenever they entered or left the department. The employees, of course, might think I was doing this because I wanted to micro-manage them, but I was willing to take that risk.

Even if they did not want to talk to me, I would still be visible. This idea was a huge culture shift for the employees, and more than a little scary to many of them, to be honest.

Since my manager did not have a budget for providing me with a new office, I convinced her to allow me to remodel an office which was central to the department. The only stipulation was that I had to agree to, was making it into a "suitable" office for a manager.

If anyone is wondering why I thought this move would build trust and communication with my employees, the answer is: I had no idea. What I *did* know, was that they would see me more than they ever saw the previous manager. And during those brief encounters there could be opportunities to build relationships and, hopefully, even begin to build a foundation of trust.

I was just taking one simple step at a time without any guarantees. This also aligned with my core value of making sure that whatever you are doing, do it for the right reason. Do it, and move forward!

A funny thing happened while remodeling this office. I was told that the door had not come in, and they were not sure when it would.

That was fine with me—and I had some fun with it, calling myself the "No-door Policy" manager, during a time when the big deal in leadership was the "open-door policy." I am sure all of you remember this management stage. It was common for managers to often use this phrase, even if they didn't practice it. I decided to take this idea to the next level.

Not having a door, meant my door was literally always open when the employees passed by during the day. Since I placed my desk so that it faced the door, practicing deliberate leadership, I trained myself to look up from my desk every time that someone did walk by. A simple behavior change on my part!

Over a period of time, the employees began to stop, ask me when I was going to get a door and at times would attempt a brief conversation. This was a huge success! The no-door opportunity turned out to be a huge communication technique, providing much more communication with the employees than I'd had with them up to that point.

When my door actually arrived, I had begun to build such a trusting relationship with employees, that I initially decided not to put the door on my office. Over time, I was forced to put the door on my office and just kept it open, holding my more serious meetings in the department conference room.

How simple is that solution to building a trusting relationship with employees? I moved my location and then made the most out of the opportunities that this small decision afforded me! So many times as a leader if I was doing something for the right reason I would get so much more than I ever expected in terms of opportunities to build trust.

Leadership Learning

I could have sent a thousand emails a day to the department and held a thousand staff meetings and not have created such a strong, trusting relationship with every employee in such a short period of time as the location of my office and the lack of a door provided.

Begin every day with your core values and how you want to influence every employee in the entire department that you are responsible for. Then do what is right and free up your thinking in terms of how to make all of that happen!

In the end, we completely turned around the department's devastating performance. In fact, it is still going strong to this day!

Stop for a Moment*

Take a minute to think about what you would have learned in any of these situations that were presented in this parable? What simple decision(s) could you make today that would, over time, build a more trusting relationship and increase communication with your employees?

_____

_____

_____

_____

KEY POINT

Make management fun again! Engage your staff in thinking about those challenges that you are facing today in a more creative and simpler way. Most of the decisions that helped me transform challenging departments came from simple, inexpensive ideas. Think about what the right thing to do is and go from there. I don't believe that innovation is a gift for the few, but it is a practice that anyone can engage in and make happen! You are more innovative than you might think.

PARABLE SIX

Get Back to Relationships

If there is one thing that I could identify as a major contributor both to ineffective communication, and driving wedges between relationships in business, it would be advances in technology, specifically, the over use of email. But I have good news: applying the message in this parable will change your business relationships within a month of changing your behavior. I can guarantee this result because in managing hundreds of employees over the years, this personal behavior change has *never failed*.

A common goal in customer service is to always be better than any other company in your field. This is not a showstopper. The showstopper is being *considered* better in relationship building than any other company by those who count—your customers, patients and clients.

We can all agree that in order to accomplish this, your staff would have to be actively engaged, considered excellent at communicating, and capable of building trust in customer relationships.

The challenge in becoming good at communication and building trust in professional relationships seems to be time. Because of corporate parameters and expectations, employees in general, especially those in leadership, are currently overwhelmed by their jobs.

Have you ever heard that complaint from your employees or managers? I have, for well over two decades. We all have too much on our plates, but technology has admittedly helped with this time challenge. We are now able to communicate with each other numerous times a day without much effort. Our communication frequency is awesome—so why aren't our relationships improving?

Through a number of sessions with my staff, I realized that our reputation was not as good as it could be with some of the other departments within our organization. In fact, there were some employees that felt we were somehow privileged within the company and worked inside a different set of guidelines.

Frankly, this particular fact didn't seem to really upset any of my staff. They claimed that these particular company employees were immature, jealous, and just unhappy people overall. The consensus was that they had always been that way and would probably never change.

Because I noticed over time that these relationships were not necessarily getting any better, I began to assess a few of my staff's emails that I was being copied on as their manager. I was surprised to discover some of the confrontational words being used. Some of the emails went back and forth, continually making the decision process longer, while accusations became more and more personal, often with challenging terminology.

Please take a minute to consider any email communications which you have recently read where the resolutions or decision-making process became somewhat convoluted and difficult to resolve. What was actually being accomplished? What do you think about this? What did you do? How would you address my situation?

_____

_____

_____

_____

In discussing this situation with my staff, I asked if they thought it was critical to build strong relationships, not only with our customers, but within our organizations as well. The general consensus was that it would be nice, but "you can't change some people" and the "staff aren't miracle workers." None of them felt responsible for the poor behavior of other company employees.

So, I decided to play the previously discussed "the boss card." I firmly believe that there are times when, as the manager, you need to make a decision, and then require that your staff follows your request. No substitutions, no discussion.

As a side note, I could go on about the application of the "boss card" since it became a fantastic tool, but it's enough to say I have never had this approach back-fire on me. In fact, I have been more respected because my staff knows exactly what to expect from me in difficult situations.

It has been my experience that employees will respect you more when they clearly understand where you stand on their behavior, based on your core values and departmental policies. This takes the guesswork and surprises out of their job. They need to know where they have wiggle room and where they do not. Wishy-washy managers are a dime-a-dozen and employees *never* respect them, because of their lack of effective leadership.

My boss card in this situation was that everyone should stop utilizing emails in order to resolve departmental conflicts, no matter how minor the conflict was. That included working within our team that also included me.

I also thought this would be a good idea, if possible, when working with customers. Today, of course this would also include the use of computer technology, but still require face-to-face communication.

I announced that I would meet with everyone on the staff after thirty days, and we would discuss this new policy, the results, and impact of this change in behavior.

To be brief, after 30 days, *every single staff member* reported that resolving a conflict situation with the person they had dealt with was more successful than they had ever imagined. It really did make a difference in the relationship and the outcome.

LEADERSHIP LEARNING

What I learned was, as professionals, we want to be valued above everything else! We go through life, little by little, in our fast-paced, productive, time-saving society unwittingly devaluing each other every day.

The fact is, we don't always care about the feelings of others. After all, we have work to get done, and money to make, and successes to be achieved.

The funny thing is that there is more success to be gained by valuing each other than by devaluing each other. When we take relationship short-cuts, we are really working against ourselves in the long run even though we are saving time.

Do you have the time to lose customers and have those that complete your work resent you internally and in silence?

As an added benefit, after we instituted the change, we were much more respected overall. As professionals, my staff was very pleased with that particular outcome of the change in policy!

What was I Doing — or Not Doing?

- I took a stand that actively creating healthy, strong, supportive relationships with departmental employees and external customers was not an option.

- I modeled deliberate leadership by not taking the easy path of assuming that email was the only way to communicate when there was conflict.

- I taught the staff how powerful and productive excellent internal customer service, as well as external customer service, could be.

- I taught that in my department, emails are not a substitute for building in-person personal and professional relationships.

- I also demanded that, in our department, we would manage technology and not let it manage us.

- As professional adults we want to be valued in our organization. This feeling of being valued does not come only from management—it comes from everyone we work with.

- A strong leader needs to be consistently and deliberately setting the ground rules for the culture that they want to create in their department.

- Life lessons, especially those about developing strong, healthy relationships, need to be brought into the workplace.

- Don't ever accept a work environment or culture that is less than you desire it to be just because everyone *else* agrees with it.

- Leadership is about motivating and helping others become the person they truly want to be in life— and you need to help get them there. This includes other employees in your organization, in addition to external customers.

STOP FOR A MOMENT

Take a moment to think about and write down other examples where technology has taken the place of personally developing relationships, and might be having a negative impact on your customer or employee relationships.

What do you think your current reputation is as a department with internal customer service? Are other departments talking negatively about working with you in the organization? Would other departments rather go around you?

_____

_____

_____

_____

KEY POINT

Strong leaders understand the value of developing and protecting their internal relationships. You can be the most efficient manager in your organization, and still not have the level of employee trust and engagement required to create a highly performing department.

PARABLE SEVEN

Conflict is a State of Mind

Over the years I have asked thousands of adult professionals if they thought conflict was negative. Seven out of ten of those adults answered *yes* to this question.

For many years this was a challenge for me as a Manager of Training, responsible for the skills and management training for thousands of employees. Handling conflict was a critical, essential step in building high performing teams in all of our training programs.

It seemed that even though we taught team building skills and conflict resolution, management and employees would still do everything they could to avoid engaging in any sort of conflict.

When I was a young thirty-year-old Dean of Student Affairs for a college in the Midwest, I was responsible for student discipline. I learned over the years that I could accept removing a student from the college because, as I was told by the former dean, I did not have the authority to waive the consequences of a student's negative behavior. At this point in my career, this made sense to me—even though the student and their parents often blamed me for the dismissal.

If conflict is acceptable, and even a positive step in building high performing teams, then why is it so difficult for leaders to have a conversation when an employee is not performing? I am told by many adult professionals that the reason they do not hold their employees accountable is because they are afraid of conflict.

STOP FOR A MOMENT

Take a minute and assess your feelings about conflict and the role it currently plays in leadership. Is it positive or negative? Are you so fearful of conflict that it keeps you from holding employees accountable for their job responsibilities? Or from removing one of your employees?

_____

_____

_____

_____

I've faced many situations when I needed to discipline employees for their performance. One day, before putting my employee "Tim" on discipline, I wondered why *I* felt so bad that *he* was not performing.

I realized at that point, that I felt like his lack of commitment was somehow my fault.

I thought back to my college dean days and the fact that I was defining this conflict as negative. So, what were the facts in this situation?

Fact: I was paying an employee to complete a certain amount of work.

Fact: This employee, who agreed to do a certain amount of work for me for that amount of money, was not doing everything he said he would do.

Fact: The company instructed me to find someone who *would* do that amount of work for that amount of money, and I was under this obligation to the organization.

Fact: I needed to find out why the work was not being completed, and whether Tim intended to do the entire job which he was hired to do.

I then realized that this was nothing more than a meeting to discuss who I was going to get to do the entire job for the money that the organization was willing to pay. All of a sudden, I realized that the conflict in this situation did not need to be negative—it was actually neutral and very straightforward.

STOP FOR A MOMENT

Take a minute and think about how you would conduct a meeting with an under-performing employee. Write out the steps and main points in the conversation you would have with this employee. Are you seeing this as a negative confrontation? Think about your feelings about this meeting and why you might be afraid about finding out if your employee is still willing to do the job they were hired to do.

_____

_____

_____

_____

At the first meeting I simply handed Tim the job description, which he was given when we met in his interview, and asked him if he remembered being given this job description. Tim said no, he hadn't seen it before.

I didn't confront him, since I could not prove that Human Resources had shown him a specific copy of this job description. Instead, I asked Tim if he remembered how much he was being paid in his current position. He said he did remember that.

I asked Tim to take the job description home and read it carefully, explaining that it was the Human Resources job description for his current position. Before he left my office, I told him that my responsibility was to find someone that could do the entire job, and for the money the organization was willing to pay.

I stated that I hoped Tim would be that person, but if he was not, I would need to find someone who would be willing to fill the position. I smiled and shook Tim's hand and asked if he understood. He said he did.

At the second meeting, I greeted Tim, and we chatted a little, before I asked if he was interested in continuing to work in his position, after studying the job description. He said yes. I told him that that sounded good, and mentioned that if he didn't complete all the job's responsibilities in the future, we would need to meet again to discuss other options. No conflict. Problem solved.

In a similar situation, where I knew the employee *had* been given the job description, and we already had one conversation about not doing the entire job, the conversation went a little differently.

During the first meeting I handed the job description to the employee, and this time I highlighted the areas of the job description which were not being completed. I asked "Sally" if she remembered our previous meeting, when we discussed her doing the entire job, and she said she would do the job going forward? Sally said she remembered.

At this point I stated once again that the entire job needed to be completed by someone, and that I was hoping that someone would be Sally. If not, I would need to fill the position with another employee. Sally was clearly shocked, and argued with me about why she *had not* been doing the entire job.

I listened to what she had to say, and then told her that I would give her sixty days to show me that she wanted the position, and could complete all the responsibilities. We would not meet again until that time unless she asked.

I told Sally that if she did not adequately fulfill the requirements of the job in that time, that I would start her on the organization's "discipline train." She would go through Human Resources' Discipline Steps which could eventually end in dismissal.

I repeated that I hoped she would stay, but at this point it was totally up to her. Then I documented the conversation.

STOP FOR A MOMENT

Take a minute and reflect on what you think was good about this process and what was not. Think about who is responsible for the employee's future employment at this point: the leader or the employee? Who will be responsible if the employee is eventually let go?

_____

_____

_____

_____

Leadership Learning

There were so many things that I learned from this process. The first was that I needed to change my thinking and perspective about conflict when discussing an employee's performance.

What many famous leadership authors have learned is that what we call conflict and discipline—and all feel negative about—are in reality just having constructive, direct, and supportive conversations with another adult concerning their previous performance commitments to the organization.

If this becomes a negative interaction, that is the fault of leadership. I have found that over the years, employees want an honest, caring, and authentic leader whom they can trust, and respect the interaction because the leader took the time to address the employee's work potential.

A manager will never be considered a leader if they can't have an adult conversation with their employees, one which will elevate their employees to a higher level of performance. This will require honest discussion about an employee's overall performance; continually!

Holding others accountable for the performance level which they committed to when they were hired, is the only way to create a culture of top performers.

When you confront an employee concerning your job expectations, this does not have to be a negative interaction. On the contrary, it can be a positive review of job expectations, to assure that you and your employees are on the same page.

These conversations should also include an overview of what the person is doing well, and where they have become more proficient. You cannot build a high performing team without having many, many of these clarifying conversations throughout a long-term employee's career.

What was I Doing — or Not Doing?

- I was willing to change my perspective of conflict and view it as constructive and necessary; not destructive.

- I respected my staff enough to challenge them to another level of performance.

- I put the responsibility of employee performance and engagement on the employee and didn't allow it to become my problem.

- I became proactive by regularly distributing each employee's job descriptions, and reviewing their performance throughout the year—not only once a year. I should take the surprise element out of performance conversations.

- I began to ask employees what more they wanted to do for the department, and spent less time on what they had not done the previous year.

- I also spent time asking each employee what I was doing or not doing that might be inhibiting their professional growth.

KEY POINT

Many times, as leaders we tend to underestimate the impact of our employees reaching their potential under our leadership. We either spend too much time making sure that they don't make mistakes, or we spend too much time trying to catch their mistakes. Engaged employees, in my opinion, want to be *fully* engaged in their career, but sometimes leadership gets in the way by not challenging them enough.

PARABLE EIGHT

The Impossible May Not Be Impossible

One of the most important actions a leader can take is to clearly communicate their message to all of their employees. The very best way to do this, in my opinion, is to gather them all together when the message is verbally expressed. Many departments, however, consider this an impossible task.

I was managing a large department of hourly employees where this type of meeting was believed to be totally impossible. The department was working twenty-four-seven and couldn't shut down, even for a couple of hours. So the challenge was replacing all the regular employees working during a specific two-hour shift with a smaller, replacement staff.

Where would I get all those replacement employees, and where would I get the extra funds to pay all the additional staff?

I placed a high value on accomplishing this because I wanted all the employees to hear the vision and mission of their department from the department executive herself—a leader who was extremely competent, but judged unfairly, and I often found myself defending her actions.

I was willing to put the program together, be the moderator for the meeting, and take care of all the logistics. For many on my staff, this became the "impossible dream."

The biggest problem that I dealt with was this "impossible" mind set. The statement that *it can't be done* was universal both within my staff, and with a few very experienced managers in the organization. It is amazing to me how years of experience can often be a manager's biggest barrier in becoming successful. Many in management seem to believe that they can't do what's never been done.

STOP FOR A MOMENT

Take a minute and think about a time when others thought a situation you were in, at work, was impossible and that you should give up. Was it really impossible? Write down your thoughts.

_____

_____

_____

_____

The idea of a departmental meeting, involving all employees and those in supervision, occurred to me during a time when turnover in the department was at an all-time high and I was trying to figure out ways to encourage and motivate everyone.

So many times, when you are in a leadership position, others will not agree with what you want to accomplish. They will tell us that our ideas are unreasonable and totally impossible. Even our executive management might balk because what we desire to do would be too much extra work and mess up the budget.

The fact is that budgets and inconveniences are huge barriers to anyone's overall progress when changes need to be made. This is an unavoidable fact in management.

One day, while thinking about the turnover issue and wanting to put a spark, somehow, back into the employees and staff, I wondered where those employees went after they left my department. I decided to have a conversation with staffing and see if they could help me with this inquiry.

I was informed that many of the exiting employees did not leave the company, but took other positions within the company. Then I took that information a step further, and sought out some of those employees to ask why they decided to leave the department. The answer I received from a majority of them was that they left the department for a better opportunity, albeit within the company.

I discovered from the current managers of those employees that the majority were considered very qualified employees, because of everything they learned about the company after working in a foundational segment of the company: the phone center.

This started me thinking again about my crazy all-department meeting idea, and how I might leverage this already trained human capital. I played the *What If* game with myself: What if those past employees missed working in their previous department? What if they were still friends with current employees whom they once worked with in that department?

Most importantly: Would those past employees like an opportunity to get back together with their old friends?

Then came the biggest *What If.*

What if I asked prior employees if they were willing to come back to the department and work for a short period of time? What if I provided free, limited training to get them back up-to-speed? Would they be open to the idea even if I could not afford to pay them? I could spring for t-shirts and some snacks in exchange for working a two-hour shift. This could be treated as an employee reunion of sorts.

My staff and I began to make calls to prior employees. We discovered that enough of them would happily volunteer their time that we could cover a two-hour shift.

To make a long story shorter, we did have our first departmental meeting, and not only was it a huge success, it was a significant step in turning the department around. I didn't even have to supply a t-shirt.

A side benefit for me was that I felt less paranoid about our department's high turnover, knowing that the employees leaving were successful contributors in the rest of the company. This started me thinking about utilizing my department as an intentional entry into the organization. But that's another story!

Never underestimate the power of ideas that can bring professional adults together. Professionals, who together, can blow the lid off of productivity, creativity, and innovation. There is nothing more powerful than a highly motivated, single-minded group of adult professionals!

On the flip side, professional adults, staff members, and managers who are driven by negative feelings about their own lives should never be given the wheel and asked to drive any organization into the future.

Remember, one drop of blue dye can impact and ruin an entire eight-ounce glass of water. Don't ever let a negative attitude ruin your dreams!

LEADERSHIP LEARNING

There are so many things that you can learn from an experience like this. First, you do not have to already be an exceptional leader to believe in what you must make happen in your department.

It is not against the law to believe that what you want to do can be powerful and inspiring. You only need to believe that what you want to do *will* be good for your department and employees. Just because you are working with some staff members that are negative does not mean that you can't make life better for everyone else.

The obvious learning in this situation is that so many things that we pass off as impossible are, in fact, possible. As I wrote in Parable Four, and experienced over the years, is that while good leadership is pretty simple, it's not necessarily easy. But that does not make it impossible.

Going against the grain of popular thinking is the toughest thing a leader and manager will ever do. But I believe that this could be one mark of an exceptional leader.

What was I Doing—or Not Doing?

- I didn't refute the negative comments concerning my idea because I knew that my idea was solid in terms of changing the old culture.

- I did continue to think about the departmental meeting goal, because my experience in previous positions taught me it would be powerful, and the quickest way to deliver a consistent message about the direction of the department.

- I thought about how this opportunity would be a powerful way for all the employees to meet and hear from our executive director in person, and realized in doing so just how competent and powerful she was.

- I did not give up on my idea, but I did not communicate that to some of my negative staff for fear of continued roadblocks being thrown in my path. Remember: good ideas do not need to be universally agreed upon to succeed.

- In terms of researching the departmental challenge of turnover with staffing, I realized that I may be able to address two problems with one solution.

- I proved that anyone can be innovative if they have the right motive and are doing what they want to do for the right reasons. Innovation is not reserved for a talented few.

- I learned once again, if anyone truly wants to be a leader, they need to demonstrate actual leadership.

There are times as a leader that the changes we need to make will take innovation—something brand-new has to be initiated by a leader who believes in the feasibility of the new thing.

This particular innovation did require a lot of courage from the leaders, mostly because those employees who had been with the company the longest, and believed they knew best were the biggest barriers to accomplishing the innovation.

A Bonus — Another Impossible idea

Another example of facing the impossible was requesting a process change with the Human Resource

Department. The fact is, in their defense, they are the staffing Gate Keepers for every organization.

In this example I was having difficulty improving the organization because we were never fully staffed. It took HR Staffing a long time to replace employees—especially if an employee quit without giving two weeks' notice.

We tried committees, teams, and employee brainstorming sessions to figure out a way to cut the replacement time down. It was very difficult for us to meet our productivity goals when we were always so short-staffed.

I am sure you have also felt this pinch in your departments. Again, the middle manager is put in the middle because on the one hand they have their manager's productivity goals to meet, but on the other hand they can't achieve them because they are not in control of staffing, the HR staffing system is.

Again, the easiest answer for past management to give was that there was no way to change the staffing process that was currently in place. It was impossible.

Stop for a Moment

Consider what you might think of doing in this situation. Is there anything that can be done? Or do you continue to use the long staffing process, which results in being short-staffed, as an excuse?

_____

_____

_____

The first thing I did in my situation was pull a diverse committee together, so I had strong company representation in the event that we could find a solution. I gathered representatives from current employees, Human Resources, the union, and my staff. We met once a week for many months, but we could not reach any real agreement.

Part of the problem was that most of the employees in the room could not believe that there really was a solution, given that what was in place had been the staffing process for years. This was *the way it had always been done.*

One day, in my own staff meeting with my supervisor, someone randomly tossed out an idea which, at the time, seemed pretty crazy. None of us initially gave it a second thought. The idea was that my staff should hire our own staff. But when this was presented at a larger task force meeting, anyone that was not part of my staff disagreed with the suggestion.

But I continued to think about the idea and, when we were in our meetings, I occasionally ran it by my staff again as a potential solution. I would make the point that while holding a brainstorming session, no idea should be labeled bad. We should just have fun with all the ideas and see where we end up.

At some point, someone asked if it would be possible for every supervisor on the staff to support the overworked HR staffing department by volunteering to interview and screen potential candidates. After we initially laughed, we started brainstorming what that process might actually look like. Why not actively support staffing when they get in a bind?

The idea that we came up with was for HR staffing to collect the resumes of potential candidates whom they would consider interviewing for our department, and then allowing us as a group to be the ones to interview those candidates.

Taking that comment a step further, given our need due to high turnover rates, we asked if it would be possible for all of us to volunteer an entire day to interview a number of candidates, and develop a matrix in terms of which ones we would suggest hiring.

We could use our workroom and post on flipchart paper the Human Resources Staffing Matrix, ranking each candidate on all the interview questions and then adding up the scores to prioritize the candidates at the end of the day.

This way, HR staffing would be able to review our recommendations and begin evaluating them the next Monday. All of a sudden, this crazy idea didn't seem so crazy. This would reduce the time required to replace department staff by half, because of the number of potential candidates the entire staff could interview in one day.

The short story is that even though staffing would lose some control they would still be able to review all the potential candidates before officially hiring them, so they agreed to try it. My manager—a strong leader—thought it would be worth taking a run at it, since we were all willing to dedicate an entire Saturday without receiving additional payment.

We gave it a try-and it worked. The impossible was possible. We still had to wait until the candidates were hired and completed training, but the time from an empty seat to a full seat was significantly reduced.

LEADERSHIP LEARNING

This is yet another example of what can happen when a leader brings adult professionals together who want to solve a challenge, and they never give up. It is my observation that when you use employees to solve departmental challenges, it makes them feel more fully utilized in the department and more valued.

Adult professionals want to be treated and respected *as* adult professionals and if we want to leverage diversity, improve employee engagement, and change a culture from the bottom up, sometimes we need to do the impossible. The impossible is pretty cool to change, but only true leaders know this because they are the only ones doing it.

WHAT WAS I DOING—OR NOT DOING?

- I was concerned that this challenge could not be solved and was discouraged for a long time.

- I believe that being sincere about listening to any suggestion by my staff was the key.

- I was concerned about bringing this to Human Resources, since I did not believe they would make any changes in their process, especially to trust my staff to conduct the interviews. The truth was, that they were surprisingly supportive and helpful. Don't let your biases trip up your good intentions!

- This is where a good relationship with your boss can pay dividends; he was a true leader.

- You need staff members who trust and believe in your vision for the department, and believe that you are always looking out for every employee.

- If you are in middle management you will need to be strong sometimes in terms of taking criticism, and possibly even sabotage, from your peers in management. Unfortunately, not everyone wants you to succeed.

KEY POINT

Being in management at times can be very tough. It is definitely not for the weak of heart, for sure. It is not easy to be humble and confident at the same time. You may question yourself at times and that is okay—but you must always know that you are doing the right thing for the right reasons. Caring about others is always the priority in any difficult situation. You are responsible for the lives of those you supervise in terms of their future well-being and careers. This is a heavy load to carry, but you can do it.

PARABLE NINE

Making the Big Bucks

The fact is, those in leadership positions, especially those in middle management, are not making a lot more money than those who report to them, especially considering the hours spent trying to do all the things that are written about in this book.

In addition, many of us have reported to managers who were not good leaders and have done more harm to our departments than good. Often this is because they didn't believe that it was worth the extra effort, given what they were being paid.

It seems to me that most of the good leadership in the world comes from individuals who truly care about enabling others to live a better life, no matter where they are working. To be honest, "leadership" isn't a position, and being in management doesn't automatically make anyone a "leader."

But I don't believe everyone needs to be a "leader" to be a good manager over a department. Managing a department or an organization is a serious job, and one that should be done well. No employee will ever be considered a leader by others unless they are first a good manager. I have worked with many excellent managers in my career, but not all of them influenced me or others as a leader.

As stated earlier, I do believe that to be recognized by others as a leader requires a higher level of engagement, commitment and extra time. I have stated many times to those whom I've taught, and to those whom I've chosen to lead, that throughout my professional career I have only reported to two managers who discussed my leadership behaviors in a performance review. *Two*.

Outside these two managers, the only criteria I have been evaluated on is *how* I managed my department, and whether I met—or did not meet—organizational objectives. Few managers have ever cared how I achieved organizational goals, they just wanted results.

This is one explanation of why there are so many in management who are arrogant bullies, and why so few employees trust or respect those to whom they report. Don't take my word for this, just ask your peers.

Of course, many employees make the managers *believe* they are trusted and respected in order to get a promotion or a raise from that supervisor, but they never consider those managers actual "leaders." (This is probably the reason bars created post-workday "happy hours"—so all of us could tell the truth about our management!)

Nevertheless, I still believe it remains true that employees primarily leave their jobs because of bad management by their direct supervisor or manager.

When I am teaching leadership in my masters and doctoral programs, I tell the students on the first night of class that I am going to present information which I hope will encourage them to choose one of the following paths:

- Become a *true leader* for the first time in their current management position.

- Become a *better leader* in their current management position.

- Make the decision to *never* go into management.

- *Get out* of management all together, and spare the lives of those they are managing.

Leaders who are passionate and deliberate about leadership—and truly care about those who work for them—constantly motivate their staff to push themselves and grow their individual productivity.

The leader does this, so that all of their employees can develop a vision for higher levels of performance, ultimately experiencing their full potential. The key for all of this to happen is that the leader needs to understand what that potential is for each of their staff.

As suggested earlier, asking employees for a professional resume is a great place to begin. By doing this, you are sending the message to everyone in your organization that if they work with you, then reaching their potential is not an option, but is expected. It also tells staff that they will be fully valued and utilized under your supervision.

True leaders strive for compassionate and quality care for all of their staff. As they grow in their leadership role, they begin to look toward their own potential as a leader and recognize the potential of others along the way. This caring leader is then able to identify and maximize potential in their staff, which leads to success for the staff, unit, facility, company and even for themselves.

Leading by mentoring and developing can be exactly what your staff needs to motivate and engage them in your department or organization. I have found that if you find the passion in your staff, and then capitalize on that passion to escalate the work being done, there is no limit to what you can accomplish together as a team.

This is not a new thought. I believe that most of us understand the logic that if we care more and give more to our employees, then they will give more back in return.

There are times when those of us in management joke about the tough decisions and personnel challenges that we have to deal with by saying, "That's why we make the big bucks." There were many times when I began a new position where, not only was I new to the operation, but I had not even met the staff who would be reporting to me. As you may know, it can take months, even years, to cultivate a trusting and committed staff.

In one particular case, the environment was one where past employee experiences with management had been anything but positive. This increased the already stressful situation of me managing an operation where I had absolutely no previous experience, and frankly made me question why I chose to be in management.

As mentioned before, one of my big ideas when I was in this position was to schedule a three-hour meeting with each of those reporting directly to me *before* I started work as their manager. To be effective leaders, we need to care about adult professionals, even if we have not yet met. These situations are calculated risks, for sure!

We might also find ourselves questioning being in leadership when we are standing up for our ideals, alone, against a higher authority. This is when we question if we actually are making the Big Bucks—and if it's worth it.

An example of this was when my department was running well and making significant change, and we had a real opportunity to become a huge success. Consequently, I was asked by my manager and Human Resources to consider bringing "William" onto my staff as a supervisor, because he did not have a "home" in the organization.

What I discovered during the meeting was that William was not a strong performer in the organization, and Human Resources wanted to remove him from his current position. This was a tough meeting for me because, although William was a nice person, few in the meeting understood how serious and important it was to have a highly performing supervisory staff when completely turning around the performance of a department. Total change really takes a firm commitment and tons of time.

STOP FOR A MOMENT

Take some time to consider what you might be thinking in this type of situation given your core values? What might be your decision?

_____

_____

_____

_____

I was able to put off agreeing to hire William during the meeting, because the primary point in my argument was that I needed a supervisor who would be an extremely high performer and a respected employee by their peers in that position. There was nothing personal in the decision. We were developing a best-in-class department, and William didn't fit that description. My manager, even though Human Resources did not agree, trusted me enough to support my decision.

I have had to make many difficult decisions throughout my twenty-four years of leadership. Decisions which were in direct conflict with other departments were the toughest ones. This is where I had to put my core values to the test and find out if I was able be the leader I wanted to be.

Leadership Learning

The biggest learning in this situation was that leadership does have a price. If you truly believe in your core values, if you believe in creating a winning environment which enables your employees to achieve their potential, and if you believe in the culture you are developing for everyone in your department, then at some point you will probably pay for it.

There will be others in your organization who will not want you to be successful, including other organizational departments. What others only care about is solving the challenges and problems that *they* are facing, even if it means taking you down. Everyone has heard the statement that "if you can't stand the heat, stay out of the kitchen." It sure does seem appropriate for leadership.

What was I Doing — or Not Doing?

- Admittedly, there may be times when it's better to adjust your immediate plans to keep the peace with other departments and your boss. But at other times we do need to give it our best shot and stay true to our core values.

- I was not willing to give up my beliefs concerning excellence and creating a staff that was in line with my vision and mission for the department.

- I was willing to take a hit on my reputation from another department in order to develop a best-in-class department, and eventually it was worth it. After the success of this department, I took a better position—with what turned out to be the best job of my professional career.

- I earned the respect of my staff after they discovered what I had done. They were thrilled with my commitment.

- I took another step in realizing how important it was for me to know who I wanted to be as a leader and the legacy I wanted to leave my current organization.

KEY POINT

Ok, so maybe we aren't making the big bucks, given all the effort, commitment, and time that we are giving to our organization. This is why it is so important for us to know *why* we are going into management and leadership, and who we are going to be when we get there. At some point in your career you will question that decision, and will want to have the right answer when you do!

If we are all to succeed, we must believe in ourselves and our decisions with our careers!

PARABLE TEN

Building Relationships that Last

While working in management and leadership for over thirty years, directing significant change in multiple departments, motivating professionals in Egypt and Japan, and teaching adult professionals at five major universities, I have made some very interesting discoveries concerning leadership.

The one thing that stands out, which seems like a simple concept for success, is to develop mature, adult relationships with your employees which you will subsequently be able to count on for the long term. It is about employees becoming committed as much to you as they are to their job.

It is my belief that ineffective managers and leaders are, for some reason, afraid to develop the kinds of relationships with their employees that they would accept as normal in their personal lives. For example, they understand that holding others accountable and resolving conflict is a normal part of any mature adult relationship.

These are the kinds of respectful relationships that they covet. Why then, when working and managing employees, are they fearful of forming the same type of trusting relationships at work?

The challenge is that, over the years, being in a management position has changed in terms of managing employee relationships.

Like most other companies, when I was the manager of training and development, we had a workshop on basic management which was called Basic Management (I took credit for the clever name).

This was exactly what it sounded like—a course covering basic concepts such as staffing, discipline, communications, training, payroll, employee relations, etc. This was many years ago, and at that time we made a big deal about "not knowing your employees on a personal level." We wanted the relationship between managers and their employees to be focused on the job and nothing else.

If the employee was having personal challenges, the manager was to refer them to the Human Resources Department as soon as possible and not become involved in any way. Today, the line has become blurred in terms of management being able to work with an employee on some of their personal as well as professional challenges.

I would propose that it is almost impossible *not* to know what is going on in an employee's life, regardless of how much we try to remain oblivious. I firmly believe that when we transition into management, it is imperative that we adjust our friendship relationships with our peers to make sure that they understand that we are now, also, their manager. This can be a tough transition which, unfortunately, many don't handle well.

I had been a manager for a short period of time over a particularly large department, and I was still trying to develop trust with all the employees. In doing this I spent a ton of time with the employees in conversations, meetings, lunches, and even the occasional "happy hour."

During this time, "Chris" had a supervisor role in my department, which meant that I saw him more often than the average employee. Over time, I could tell that Chris was not happy in my department.

I constantly wondered what to do about him, because his discontent was impacting his job performance. Should I be truthful? Should I confront Chris in terms of what I was seeing in his behavior? More to the point —should I be the one to talk to him about what was going on in his current situation, or should I notify Human Resources and have them get involved?

The twist here was that Chris and I did not have a good relationship. In fact, I would go so far as to say that Chris did not like me. The relationship was stretched, for sure.

STOP FOR A MOMENT

Take some time and write down what you might have done in this situation. Would you confront this employee? How might you address the issue, if you feel that you should? How risky is this situation in terms of the long-term relationship since this employee is in a leadership role?

_____

_____

_____

_____

It is always a risk, as manager, when confronting one of your employees about their performance in the department. If you have been in management for a while, you understand that something like this could blow up in your face, and that is why many in management do nothing.

But I knew that if I did nothing, my inaction would negatively impact the department, other employees, and my ability to change a culture which was full of disengaged employees. To muddy the waters further, would Chris feel that by confronting him about his personal feelings about the job, be crossing some kind of line regarding employee/manager relations?

I decided to invite Chris into my office and confront him. I was hoping that I had built up enough trust with him, that he would see that I was only trying to help.

I told Chris that I couldn't help but notice that he appeared unhappy in his work, and with the company, and that his discontent was impacting not only his performance, but also his influence on his staff. Dead silence filled my office. I wasn't prepared to say anything more than this, and didn't know where I would to go in the absence of a response.

Chris pulled a deep sigh, then asked if it was that obvious. I said yes. He then began to relate all the things that had happened in his professional and personal life, and admitted that he was very unhappy and had been for a long time.

During the conversation Chris explained what he wanted to do with his life and, since he couldn't be in the career of his choice, he decided to take a leadership position in the department. He also admitted that he needed the money.

I wanted to be totally honest, so I told Chris that I thought it would benefit us both in the long run if he rethought his position in the department since he was not committed either to being a leader, or to working to change the current culture. The bottom line was: if he couldn't be a positive influence in doing his job, he could lose it.

We also discussed how difficult it would be for Chris to get a position in the career of his choice, based on what he would have to accomplish. He told me he had one year left to finish his education, and then he would like to look for a different position within the same company.

I offered Chris a compromise: if he would give me one-hundred-percent at work, then I would let him schedule time to finish his education. Also, since I was a manager, I had contacts within the company and would help him look for another position.

The short story is that he agreed, finished his education and took a job in the same company in his chosen field.

This is called a win-win. I got rid of a disengaged supervisor—and he got rid of me *and* a job that was messing up both his personal and professional lives. Better yet, he stayed with the company!

LEADERSHIP LEARNING

This is a great lesson in terms of why being a Leader is so much more powerful than just managing a department. While management is about accomplishing goals and objectives, leadership is about having an influence in a persons' life. It is my bias that one of the most important functions of a strong leader is developing employees into their full professional potential.

I remembered an old principle I used to teach from Zig Zigler when we were using his motivational training program. He would tell us, "You will get what you want, if you help others get what they want." From that point on, Chris gave me one-hundred-percent every day, and I had plenty of lead time in hiring his replacement.

I don't understand why we, in management, don't spend more time, taking the time, to really establish strong, professional relationships with all of our employees. It is always a win-win! What are we so afraid of? What is so terrible about telling the truth about what is happening in the workplace?

What was I Doing — or Not Doing?

- I did not jump on the employee the minute that I thought I was not getting one-hundred-percent from him.

- I assessed the situation and made sure that the timing was right for me to confront the employee in what was a very sensitive situation.

- I decided that my primary goal should be to save the relationship and build respect, not destroy the little respect that he might have had for me.

- I decided in advance that I was going to tell the truth and be firm in terms of a resolution.

- I also decided that Chris was basically a good employee and might just be in the wrong position (this is the case with so many good employees that are not performing well). Finding a good fit is crucial when you are staffing!

- I knew that whatever happened I would be modeling my leadership in terms of addressing and handling employee conflict.

Key Point

The "Thirty-thousand Foot" lesson for me, also known as the "Big Picture," is simple: leaders build powerful organizations in small steps. This is why you must Build Relationships that Last! Being intentional and deliberate with every person, every decision, every situation, and every conversation is crucial if you want to build something amazing and create a high performing department that will last a lifetime! So many in management think that they can just go to work daily and come up with solutions to challenges without knowing what they are committed to doing in and for their department.

As mentioned many times before: You need to Know Yourself First and then Design a Culture that Models those Core Values!

Closing Thoughts

Over the years I have discovered some very normal, mature, relationship characteristics that need to be a part of being an effective leader. I collected these while being a Corporate Leader and Adjunct Faculty over a 30-year period. These cost me a ton of time, dedication and commitment to learn:

- Develop an honest, open, and authentic relationship with your employees. Game-playing and organizational surprises should be minimized, and everyone should be expected to take responsibility for their own behavior, decisions, and consequences.

- Employee discussions concerning both good and bad performance are expected at any time, and not held only once a year in a performance review.

- Conversations about being a best-in-class department or organization are ongoing, with new goals being set whenever current ones are reached.

- Employee feedback is respected and acted upon, even when it provides a diverse perspective.

- Leaders are not fearful of making a bad decision, and can expect the support of employees in reversing any decision that was made if necessary.

- Conflict is seen as a natural part of any relationship and developing a team, and is treated as such.

- Bullying is never an acceptable way of treating anyone in the organization.

- The way that leadership treats everyone in the organization should be consistent, never situational.

- Good leaders decide and predetermine how their daily behavior as a leader will best motivate and enable their employees to reach their individual potential.

- Good leaders are not "lucky" in terms of getting superior performance from their employees. Their behavior towards their employees is consistently deliberate and predetermined for a desired outcome, every single day. As a result, they have fewer disengaged staff.

- Good leaders model the behavioral outcome that they desire. Because they don't overreact to current employee or team behavior which they observe, that calmness and confidence allows them to manage employees to the best of their ability.

STOP FOR A MOMENT

List some of the things you have learned about leadership. What are the deliberate and intentional characteristics and behavior you can be committed to as a leader? Write them down.

_____

_____

_____

_____

An interesting conversation you might want to have with your staff is to ask them to list the qualities which they think determines a leader.

Take it a step further and ask what they would like to communicate to you in terms of your leadership. This can be a powerful conversation if you are not too risk aversive! Be brave. Begin being the leader you want to become.

Over the years the list that I gathered that came from these conversations with staff include:

- Get out of the way.

- Be available.

- Move more decisions to a lower level.

- Live up to your promises.

- Quit trying so hard to be the boss.

- Deliver what you say you are going to deliver.

- Communicate important information about the employee's future as soon as possible.

- Give up some of your control.

- Trust us; you hired us.

- Be more of a leader and less of a friend.

- Confront poor employee behavior.

- Lead by example.

- Be ethical.

- Hold everyone accountable.

- Demand excellence.

KEY POINT

The fact is, not one of us are perfect at leadership. As mentioned before, I am not the only one that supports the theory that good leadership is more of an art than a science. We can use a systems approach to managing our department or organization, but when it comes to motivating and changing the behavior of employees, this is where the art of the relationship begins.

I will conclude my parables in the same way that I began. The starting point, and key component, to Life Changing Leadership is to know and understand: Who You Want to Be as Leader. It's all about you!

About the Author

Dr. Retts has spent the last 30 years involved in leadership. His goal has been to develop organizations into best-in-class operations, while improving employee attitude, morale, and organizational loyalty.

His passion has been to influence and develop professional adults in a way that would increase their effectiveness as leaders and greatly improve the overall quality of their personal and professional lives.

Dr. Retts has worked in leadership positions that included Supervisor of Corporate Training and Development and Skills Training, Manager of Residential Services, Manager in Commercial Customer Services and Dean of Student Affairs.

Dr. Retts has also been active in the past thirty years teaching doctoral, masters and under-graduate level leadership and management related courses as an adjunct faculty for seven universities and one community college.

Published leadership articles include: "While the Cat's Away, Will the Mice Play?" and "I'm Too Nice? Caring Leaders Are Often Misjudged."

Dr. Retts' international experience includes developing a two-week Management Development Seminar for the Ministry of Public Works and Water Resources Department in Egypt and two years of

It's All About You!

Communications Training for National Panasonic in Tokyo and Osaka, Japan.

Schedule a free 45-minute consultation to discuss your specific challenges and potential solutions—no obligation or pressure tactics. I. Opportunities are only accepted if there is a strong fit for success.

Visit the website at http://www.RettsMMM.com.

Email the author at crretts@gmail.com